Writers
in the
Schools

Writers in the Schools

A Guide to Teaching
Creative Writing
in the Classroom

Susan Perabo

University of Arkansas Press
Fayetteville   1998

02 01 00 99 98   5 4 3 2

Designed by Liz Lester

☉   The paper used in this publication meets the minimum
requirements of the American National Standard for
Permanence of Paper for Printed Library Materials Z39.48-
1984.

Library of Congress Cataloging-in-Publication Data

Perabo, Susan, 1969–
     Writers in the schools : a guide to teaching
creative writing in the classroom / Susan Perabo.
          p.   cm.
     ISBN 1-55728-492-X (pbk : alk. paper)
     1. Creative writing—Study and teaching.
2. English language—Composition and exercises.
3. School prose, American—Arkansas.   4. School
verse, American—Arkansas.   I. Title.
PE1404.P39   1998
808'.042'07—dc21   97-39768
                                         CIP

Acknowledgments

Thanks first to the schoolchildren across Arkansas who have made the Arkansas Writers in the Schools program a successful and rewarding endeavor, and to the University of Arkansas for its long-standing support of the program. Also, thanks to Miller Williams, director emeritus of the University of Arkansas Press, for recognizing that the teaching methods which have been so successful in the Arkansas program could be of great use to educators across the country.

This book would not have been possible without the help of scores of staff members from Arkansas Writers in the Schools over the past twenty-five years. I wish to especially thank Sha'an Chilson, Jay Karr, and Susan Maertz for their assistance in helping to create and compile many of the exercises in this book. Thanks also to J'laine Robnolt, Beth Ann Fennelly, Katrina Vandenberg, Sha'an Chilson, Donald Justice, and the many Arkansas students whose fine work is included in the following pages.

Finally, my gratitude goes to James Whitehead, for his invaluable help with this book and for his three decades of enthusiastic leadership in the Arkansas Writers in the Schools program. Over the years he has helped so many of us realize that the mark we as writers leave in the classroom is at least as important as the mark we leave on the page; his fist-pounding has indeed inspired a generation of students to become a generation of teachers.

Contents

Introduction

Any child, at any age, has the necessary tools to be creative; imagination is a gift we are born with and a skill we can improve upon. The classroom allows teachers the opportunity to offer guidance and encouragement to students as they transform creative thinking into creative writing.

The exercises outlined in this book, although geared toward poetry and fiction, can help foster creativity in any discipline and certainly in every kind of writing. Poetry may not be a marketable skill in today's competitive job market, but creativity is, and students who understand this will have a good start in whatever they plan to pursue.

Throughout the book are poems, written by Arkansas students, which have been previously published in the yearly anthologies produced by the Arkansas Writers in the Schools program. These anthologies include *A Wild Animal Nearby* (1993), *Gone By Snowfall* (1994), and *Crossing Arkansas by Dream* (1995). Also included in the book are poems by award-winning and highly acclaimed poets, many of whom are former or current staff members of Arkansas Writers in the Schools. All unattributed poems were written by the author. In all cases, it is helpful (if not *necessary*) for students to hear this poetry *read aloud*, not simply to understand a specific exercise, but to become familiar with the music of language, a music that cannot be heard to the fullest when reading silently.

Please note, this book is divided into beginning, intermediate, and advanced exercises. However, this does not mean that the beginning section is for younger students and the advanced section is for older students. All of these exercises can be used for any age group, and, ideally, the book should be worked through from front to back.

1 ✐ Getting Started

What Is Poetry?

Pose this question to your students. If you are teaching elementary students, they will probably answer with "something that rhymes!" If you're teaching older students, they will probably groan and roll their eyes. "Boring," they will likely say, or perhaps "sappy."

Your response to all of these answers (and probably any other answer you will encounter while introducing poetry) should be the same: "Does it *have* to be?" Does it *have* to rhyme? Does it *have* to be boring? Does it *have* to be sappy? The answer, of course, is no; it doesn't have to be any of these things. It also doesn't have to be ancient, doesn't have to be about love or flowers or birthdays, doesn't have to use big words.

Simply put, poetry is language that expresses the senses. The creation of this type of imagery—imagery that expresses not only sight but also sound, touch, taste, and smell—is the poet's task and pleasure. In creating such imagery, the students express their own unique perspectives on the things about which they are writing. That *unique perspective* is the answer to the original question.

What Can Poetry Be About?

Most students, in answer to this question, will say "feelings." Feelings are a fine thing to write poetry about. But ask the students, "Can you write a poem about a cockroach? About your brother's gym socks?" The answer is yes. A poem can be written about virtually anything, as long as it effectively illustrates the writer's unique perspective.

The Six Senses

A writer expresses **senses** through language. Ask the students to list the five senses; then write them on the board. Ask which of the senses we use most often. The answer, clearly, is the sense of sight. An overwhelming percentage of all spoken description utilizes only the sense of sight. If the sense of sight is all students rely upon when writing poetry, they are limiting themselves. Have the students close their eyes and then pick up something off their desks. It may be a book, a pencil, a sheet of paper—it doesn't matter. Tell them to try to experience that object in as many ways as possible, so that they could explain it to someone who cannot see. After about a minute, have the students open their eyes. Ask a few students to describe their objects to the class, without saying what they are, and see if the rest of the class can identify the objects.

Now, ask the students what the *sixth* sense is. They will probably be confused by this question, as they have already been taught that there are five senses. And yet this sixth sense is the most important sense to use when writing poetry. What do we use, besides those five basic senses, when describing something? The answer is *imagination*. This is the sixth sense, the one which grows from the combination of all the other senses, the one which will fully allow the students' unique perspectives to be felt through their poems.

The Group Poem

A group poem combines ideas and images from as many students as possible in the classroom and is written on the board by the teacher as the students compose. In many of the exercises in this book, if not all, it is often best to start with a group poem. Being able to guide students through an exercise in this way will give you a chance to answer most of the questions and problems the students will encounter as they begin to write their own individual poems. The best way to create a group poem is simply to let students call out ideas after you explain a given exercise. Obviously, not every student's idea will be used in the group poem, but it should give each of them a chance to see, most importantly, the *form* of the poem.

Concrete/Abstract

To use their senses to the most effective degree, students of creative writing must use their ability to be **concrete** rather than **abstract**. Too often, students are encouraged to use abstractions such as "nice," "bad," or "pretty" to describe a feeling or image. In poetry, such abstractions should be set aside and replaced with more concrete language.

The following is a typical conversation that will ensue when discussing abstract terms.

Teacher: What does it mean when I say I've had a nice day?

Student: You had a good day.

Teacher: All right. What does it mean when I say I've had a good day?

Student: You had fun. You did stuff that you liked.

Teacher: What's fun to me?

Student: Stuff you like.

Teacher: What stuff do I like?

Student: Stuff that's fun.

The reason this conversation goes nowhere is that students are conditioned to speak (and sadly, often to think) in abstractions, not to consider the particulars of emotions.

Teacher: I had a nice day today. I got up at 5:30, jogged three miles, ate raw eggs for breakfast, and watched the weather channel for a half hour.

Student: What's so nice about that?

This is the point at which the pitfalls of abstract language become clear to students. The word "nice" is finally useless, because it means something different to everyone. It has no clear definition. When students try to define it, they only end up using other abstractions. In poetry, a writer must paint a picture of "nice," so that readers will understand what the writer means by the word.

Concrete words make poetry engaging. If Theodore Geisel (Dr. Seuss) had said that the Grinch Who Stole Christmas was "bad" or "mean," readers of his book may not have been interested in hearing more. But because he says the Grinch is "a three-decker sauerkraut and toadstool sandwich with arsenic sauce," readers read on.

✎ Exercise

Have students name abstract words, and list them on the board. A sample list might include these:

happy	worried
sad	hopeful
afraid	frustrated
proud	surprised
excited	disappointed

Now, instruct the students to each pick one word. Tell them it is their responsibility to save the word from being abstract, their challenge to turn it into something concrete. How is this done? By using the five senses. Here are a couple examples:

Love

A football helmet on my fourth birthday,
a silly song when I'm nervous,
Meemaw throwing kisses
as we drive away.

Mad

Mad tastes like a jalapeño pepper.
Mad looks like a burning house.
Mad feels like pine needles on bare feet.
Mad sounds like a screeching bird.
Mad smells like spilled vinegar.

This exercise should convey to the students the importance (as well as the challenge) of being concrete. Hopefully, students will also realize that it is more fun for the writer and reader to create images with concrete words.

General/Specific

General versus **specific** has much in common with abstract versus concrete, but when dealing with generalities we are often referring to groups of nouns and not adjectives. For example, a general word is "car," a specific word is "Corvette." A specific description is "a three year old blue Corvette with shiny wheels and a broken horn." Also when dealing with generalities, students must learn that a description of merely one *part* of the whole is not enough.

✑ Group Exercise

Instruct the students to close their eyes and picture a dog. Tell them to raise their hands when they can see a clear picture of their chosen dog. When all the students have a clear picture, they may all open their eyes. Pick out one student and ask for a description of the dog. If the reply is "a Labrador," push for more detail. Was it a puppy? What color was it? Did its ears stick up or hang down? After the student has completely described the dog, move to other students and have them describe the dogs they saw. Chances are that the pictures described will be completely different. Why? Because each student has a unique imagination—"dog" is not specific enough to paint a clear picture in the reader's mind.

A further way to explain this concept is to give the students a specific situation.

> **Teacher:** My sister is arriving today at the airport, but I won't be able to pick her up. One of you will have to go for me. You'll be able to recognize her because she has brown hair.
>
> **Student:** That's not enough. There might be lots of women with brown hair.

Teacher: All right. She has brown hair, and she'll be wearing a red sweater.

Student: That still isn't enough.

Teacher: What if I tell you she'll be wearing soccer cleats and a big orange hat with green polka dots? Is that enough?

Student: That's enough.

Action Verbs

By now, the students should be able to realize the importance of making adjectives concrete and nouns specific. Another important aspect of the poem is the **action verb**. In poetry, students must use action verbs to make their poems exciting.

✏ Group Exercise

Discuss boring verbs like "went" and "go." Ask the students, "What do people look like when they're 'wenting'?" Of course, there is no answer. "Went" creates no picture, so it is not an engaging word to use in a poem. Instruct the students to come up with a verb that they can act out to the rest of the class. It must be something that the class can see, hear, or feel. Here are some possibilities:

jump	stand
sit	laugh

Call on several students to act out their chosen verbs. After a few examples, students may become interested in increasingly violent action words such as "hit," "kick," and "pinch." Remind students that there are numerous peaceful possibilities:

whisper	shrug
lift	dance
hop	sing
tap	

Action verbs cause excitement, not only in a classroom but also in a poem. The students will catch on to this quickly.

Sound Poem

Poems are meant to be read aloud. This is why sound is such an important aspect of all poetry. Playing with sounds not only can be one of the most enjoyable things students of poetry do but also can be an invaluable tool in teaching the effectiveness of well-chosen words and the power of language.

In the sound poem, students will write poems made up of words with similar sounds. They may choose to use **assonance** (similar vowel sounds), **consonance** (similar consonant sounds), **alliteration** (two or more words that begin with the same consonant sound), or any combination of the three, as in the following poem.

The Queen of Cups

How still she sits amid yesterday's cups,
her breath shredding the fabric of frail steam
as her lips test the edge of plain bone china,
pale and shadowy as a paper screen.

Her words are *sacrifice, serve, succumb.*
But in the shifting surface of the tea—
that which obeys the bowl and bows to cups—
she sees the many people she could be.

Thus she slides between the painted saucers,
meanders among their delicate clinks—
this queen so perched on the brink of action,
a queen of those who'd rather hold than drink.

J'laine Robnolt
Arkansas Writers in the Schools

The first instinct the students may have in writing a sound poem is simply to *rhyme* at the close of each line. Encourage the students to use the other techniques *in addition* to rhyming, as in the example poem. Ask the students, "What are the primary sounds in 'The Queen of Cups'?" The one that stands out the most clearly is the *s*. Also, *k* sounds dominate in the last few lines. Encourage students to read this poem, and their own sound poems, aloud, even as a group: the better a sound poem is, the more fun it is to read aloud.

Simile And Metaphor

Used imaginatively, **similes** and **metaphors** can be wonderful tools in creating images in poetry. A simile is a comparison that uses "like" or "as." "She was like a beautiful swan." A metaphor does not use "like" or "as." "She was a beautiful swan." Of the two, the metaphor is stronger; the omission of "like" or "as" creates a tighter bond between the subject (she) and the image to which it is compared (swan). However, students are often more comfortable with the looser connection offered in a simile.

✏ Exercise: Making the Common Uncommon

In this exercise, encourage the students to create the most interesting, unexpected, and unique similes or metaphors they can think of for some very common things they see every day. It will be helpful to read the examples and do a group poem on the board, so that the students understand the level of imagination necessary for this poem. Simply pick three things the students see every day (or often). It is best to pick things that have many possibilities. "Book" or "pencil" doesn't make for an interesting simile. Things in nature or very large things (such as "house" or "jungle gym") work well.

Untitled

A house is like an arrow tip.
Clouds are big puffs of smoke.
A dog is like a desk with a head and a tail and secrets
  inside.

Skyler Collins
Prairie Grove, Arkansas

Untitled

Snow is white dirt falling from the sky.
Leaves are colored pieces of paper cut out like hands.
Cows are big fat bags walking in a field.

Tiffany Pershall
Prairie Grove, Arkansas

Clichés

At some point in its life, probably every **cliché** was fresh and clever; however, after years of overuse even the wittiest phrase or comparison becomes dull. When students use clichés in poetry, they are in essence saying, "I couldn't think up something on my own, so here's this old thing." This sacrifices the unique perspective that is the key to a successful poem.

✏️ Group Exercise

Ask students for the most obvious clichés to describe a certain thing. For instance, what's the first word that comes to mind when you begin the simile "white as . . ."? Most students will probably say "snow." "Different as . . ."? Usually they'll say "night and day." Have students call out alternative similes: white as vanilla yogurt, different as hawks and hummingbirds, et cetera.

Clichés can also be used in the form of ideas, and often such clichés fall into the dangerous ground of stereotyping. Going by misinformed notions that a certain group of people (or type of person) is sneaky or dirty or mean or stupid shows not only a lack of creativity but also a lack of understanding. A seemingly nonthreatening illustration of this is the way students often write about aliens. This is a topic that most young writers are fascinated by, and yet most will fall back onto the clichés of big-headed, beady-eyed Martians whose sole goal is to take over the earth. Thus, what could be an interesting and creative poem falls flat because no unique perspective is involved.

A good rule for students to go by is if they've heard it before, they should probably say something else.

Line Breaks

At this point it would be helpful to discuss **line breaks**. You may have noticed that the lines of students' poems often go all the way out to the end of a page, or that students break for a line only at the end of a sentence. Young students often have trouble understanding the concept that poetry is told in lines, not in sentences. This is one way that poetry is different from fiction.

✏ Group Exercise

A good exercise for introducing line breaks is this: Ask the students to describe something. Just point out the window and pick anything, a tree, a swing set, a car, whatever you see. Come up with a long description in the form of a sentence and write it on the board, all the way across, not breaking the line. Ask the students, "Is this a line of poetry?" The answer is yes. Now, break the line in half. Erase the second half of the sentence and rewrite it on the board under the first half. Is this poetry? Yes. Read the sentence aloud. Ask the students, "How is this different from the longer line?" Point out how the break gives special emphasis to the last word of each line, perhaps even changes the meaning of the sentence somehow. Now break the second line in half, repeating the process. Try writing the whole sentence over, breaking after every two or three words. Discuss how these changes alter the original meaning, and the feeling, of the description.

Here is an example:

I saw an oak tree with flaking bark and a yellow bird
      perched on top.

I saw an oak tree with flaking bark
and a yellow bird perched on top

I saw an oak tree with flaking bark
and a yellow bird
perched on top.

Notice how this example emphasizes the "yellow bird" by giving it its own line.

I saw an oak tree
with flaking bark
and a yellow bird perched
on top.

This variation emphasizes the "on top."

I saw
an oak tree
with flaking
bark and
a yellow
bird perched
on top.

This variation will make the reader pause on each word because the structure is so choppy.

What the students should understand from this exercise is that the way writers choose to break their lines can alter the meaning, and certainly the feeling, of a poem. Often, if a student reads the line aloud, it becomes clear where a pause should fall. Hearing their own words spoken can be an invaluable tool for the students as they grow as poets.

Prop Poems

Using **props** is an excellent way to get students focused on a topic or image. Often, having actual concrete objects in front of them will make the writing of the poems come more easily.

A simple prop exercise is to pass around a grab bag of ordinary objects—an eggshell, a remote control, a hat, a spoon—and have each student pick an object from the grab bag to write about.

A more complicated, but always successful, prop poem is the dress-up poem. Bring in a box of dress-up clothes. You may use a variety of hats, shoes, and jewelry, as well as clothing. Have the students dress up in whatever they choose from the box and then write a poem about the person who would wear the thing that they have on. If you are unable to find enough articles of clothing, you could assign the students to each bring in one garment or accessory. Pile everything together and have the students choose something other than what they brought.

The possibilities for prop poems are endless; if you have the resources and the time, props can be used in a variety of ways to promote creativity.

A Note on Revision

Often in student writing, **revision** is overlooked. Perhaps we are so thrilled to see creativity in any form that we are afraid of discouraging students by telling them to write their poems again—and make them *better!* This is a natural reaction. However, if the students are to improve as writers, they must learn to revise.

To start them on this track is simple: After they have completed an exercise, instruct them to go back to their poems and try to find one word that is abstract or general. You may have to briefly review the lessons concerning concrete versus abstract and specific versus general. Now, instruct the students to cross out *just that one word* and replace it with a word that is (or words that are) concrete or specific. In making these changes, the students have just revised their poems. If you begin this process early in the writing of poetry, students will be increasingly willing to do more major revisions. More importantly, they will see from the beginning the degree to which revision can improve their poems.

2 ✏️ Beginning

If/Were Poem

The if/were poem gives students a chance to be playful and inventive. To do this exercise you will need a package of index cards, enough so that the students can receive two cards each. On each index card, write a plural noun. It can be anything: animals, toys, kitchen utensils. The possibilities are endless:

giraffes	noodles	bubble gum
stars	earrings	snowflakes
pretzels	trucks	pencils
basketballs	cockroaches	tubas
pianos	clocks	mice

✏️ Exercise

First, do a group poem. Pick out two of the index cards. Say you choose "giraffes" and "bubble gum." Ask the students, "What would happen if giraffes were bubble gum?" This will probably fluster the students; they may think they're being tricked in some way. Tell them to use their imaginations. What would happen?

You wouldn't be able to get your mouth closed to chew.
Its head would always be sticking out of your mouth,
    looking around.

If you did get your mouth closed, the bubbles you blew
    would be yellow with black spots.
People would have giraffes stuck to the bottom of their
    shoes after recess.

Notice a few things. The most glaringly obvious effects will come first. Encourage the students to go beyond the obvious. The first two or three ideas may come in the space of a minute or two, but the more the students get into the poem the more they will have to let their imaginations really run. Push the students; given enough time, they will come up with amazing things. Now, hand out the cards and instruct the students to write their own if/were poems.

One final note, when using index cards in any exercise, the students will often want to trade cards. This is fine, but should be kept to a minimum. If you think any students truly have too tough a job with the cards they have chosen, you may give them other cards. Most of the time, though, every combination can be done well.

Through the Eyes of an Animal

This is one exercise that does not need to be done as a group poem first. All students have probably imagined what it would be like to be a certain kind of animal. This is their chance to tell others about it. They can pick any animal they wish, a domesticated pet or something more exotic—an iguana, a cougar, a blue whale. Remind the students to focus on the senses: What does the animal see, hear, smell, taste, feel?

Dolphin

Every day I jump through hoops
and dance on my tail.
The children squeal
when I splash them,
applaud when I catch the fish
in mid-air.
The water is cool and bright
and I miss the murky ocean,
miss how it feels to whip my tail
and swim as far as I can go
without running into a wall.

It is often effective to work against a stereotype in an animal poem. Tigers don't always have to be mean, nor do mice always have to be meek. Especially for older students, this simple poem offers the opportunity to look at what may be a very common sight (perhaps a cat in a window, as in the below example) in a new and intriguing way.

House Cat Geometry

I am a circle of cat
in sunlight,
tail to nose,
chin on all my paws.
In my rhombus of sun
I dream of acute angles
between hips and claws
which bring me sparrows.

I am the length of cat,
stretched flicking tail

to twitching whisker,
it takes to measure the width
of your newspaper.

I am the curl of paw
dipping into your glass,
and the arc of spine
that becomes a slope of fur.

I am the proof of forty million years
of geometric evolution, proof of Egypt,
and the properties of cats and pyramids.
Sitting still in the window of my home,
I am what is given.

Sha'an Chilson
Arkansas Writers in the Schools

Acrostics

In an **acrostic**, the first letters of the lines combine to form a word; usually, the images in the poem serve as a definition, or definitions, of that word. Acrostics are a fun and easy way for students to use specific language to describe a word. They are also a helpful exercise in dealing with line breaks. In an acrostic, the letter at the beginning of each line of poetry is a letter in the word the poet has chosen to write about. Here's an example, an acrostic about snow.

Sleepy animals
Nestle in their beds
On mountains and in valleys.
Winter is coming.

If they choose, students can use just one or two words per line.

Stillness of
November.
Owls have
White wings.

An acrostic can be written using any type of word, although often students choose a person close to them (either as a common or proper noun, "brother" or "Thomas") to begin with. Animals and hobbies are also fine topics for acrostic poems.

Portrait Poem

A portrait poem is exactly what it sounds like, a portrait of someone the student knows. It is best to encourage the students to do a member of their family; if they do a friend, the results will probably be too silly. Ideally, this poem should have eight lines. The *first line* should introduce the person and set the scene. The *following five lines* use one sense per line. The *seventh line* will show an action, and should include a simile. The *eighth line* should try to tell what the person is thinking. The following are two examples of successful portrait poems.

Untitled

My uncle is bored
He feels trapped
He smells ink from the pen
He hears people chattering outside the office
He tastes the cold leftover meat from last night

He sees papers due today
He raises his pen like a weary soldier ready for battle
He is thinking about the weekend and getting away.

Daniel Kitchens
Umpire, Arkansas

Hero

My grandfather is fighting a fire.
He feels extremely hot.
He smells smoke that seeps through the helmet.
He hears the fire scalding the building.
He tastes his sweat as it runs off his lip.
He sees a child.
He protects the child like a mother kangaroo.
He's thinking about the sun, the grass, and the things
    that he will allow that child to see again.

Jeffrey Hicks
Umpire, Arkansas

It's vital to do a group poem with this exercise, so that the students will understand the format; when done as a group poem, it essentially becomes a fill in the blank exercise. For the group poem, it's best to think of a general person to describe. A policeman, an athlete, a doctor, any of these will work and will help the students understand the format so that they can write their own poems.

Recipe Poem

A recipe poem will continue to focus on the importance of concrete and specific language. A group poem is advised here; it will help the students understand the format as well as the idea. "Fun" is a good word to use for the group poem. Ask the students, "If you had to make a recipe for fun, what would it be?" If they don't understand, ask, "Would it include six hours of school, three pages of homework, four chores?" Of course not. They will know this because they have most likely understood the lessons of concrete versus abstract and general versus specific. The following is an example of a typical recipe poem:

Recipe For Fun

Take one Saturday
add three friends
and a big blue lake.
Fifteen pieces of fried chicken,
two pounds of mashed potatoes.
Fifty worms to catch
1000 fish.

Bake until sunset.

Have students come up with other abstract words that could be written as recipes. Here are some possibilities:

love	pride
fear	surprise
anger	success

Students may also try to create recipes for people:

mother	doctor
father	teacher
grandmother	football player
grandfather	

If the students read these poems aloud, it could be interesting to have them read their works as riddles. Instruct them to leave the title out and simply read the recipe. Then let the other students try to guess what the recipe is for.

Name Poem

The name poem exercise helps young writers look at physical shapes in new and unique ways. It is a favorite among students because they get to use their own names as part of their poems, thus making the poems more personal. In the name poem, students must see letters not as letters but as shapes, pictures, images. A simple group poem, using either the name of the teacher or perhaps the name of the school or town, is very helpful in introducing the students to this concept.

Wynne, Arkansas

W is a bat flying away.
Y is a windmill with a missing spoke.
N is a Z that's asleep.
N is a clothesline that has fallen down.
E is a broken pitchfork.

Now instruct the students to write their own name poems. They can come up with one or two descriptions for each letter. Encourage them to look at the letter as a shape; let them turn it around on its side or upside down. If they are having trouble finding a description for the capital letter, they may change the letter to lowercase. Depending on the age of the students, this poem can turn out to be very simple or quite elaborate, as seen in the following examples:

Katrina

K is the shadow of a girl slumped up against a wall.

A is a tent with long, tight ropes and pins to support it.

T is a curving, iron green streetlamp to sit under and read.

R is an enormous unblinking eye with legs.

I is the edge of the rose garden's wall.

N is a cat stretching to the sun with its tail pointed at the
sky and

A is the cupboard of my brain, with its thoughts folded
inside.

The above example is an excellent name poem. But now
watch the author take it one step further:

Katrina On Dickson Street

K, the shadow of a girl slumped against a Fayetteville
wall, and

A is the tent where she sometimes sleeps outside the
city limits, with its long tight ropes and pins to
secure her to the ground.

T will be, say, the curvy iron streetlamps outside the
art center, above her as she reads and the skate-
boarders hover. To her,

R looks like an enormous, unblinking eye with legs,
who could stand on the other side of a streetlamp.
He would see the letter

I as the edge of the rose garden's wall. The eye is too
afraid to look around it. But if he did, the girl thinks
he might only find petals on cement, caterpillars, and
the letter

N, a cat stretching in the sun with its tail pointed at
    the sky.

At night, the girl folds all these thoughts away,
    in the cupboard of her brain, shaped like a capital
A.

Katrina Vandenberg
Arkansas Writers in the Schools

With students of any age, it will be best to start with the simplest version of the name poem and then, if appropriate, move on to the more ambitious possibilities.

Picture Poem

The picture poem is an excellent break for students weary of writing, especially young students, some of whom may rather draw than write. The simplest way to write a picture poem is for the students to write poems describing a certain object or animal. You may assign them all the same thing or let them pick their own. When the poems are finished, have the students draw pictures of their object or animal around the poems themselves. It can work the other way, too; if the students choose to start with pictures, they may then write the poems about the pictures inside their drawings.

Writing To Music

Although the exercises in this book allow students to "do their own thing" to some extent, writing to music will give them an opportunity to write with no (or few) boundaries. Encourage them to write whatever they wish, but to attempt to write something that they feel *fits* the music. Classical music will inspire different images and ideas than will rock-and-roll. It's also helpful to bring in types of music the students have probably never heard before, perhaps music from other countries. They needn't write *about* the music; they simply may wish to write *to* it.

3 ✏ Intermediate

Personification Poem

Personification—giving human qualities to non-human objects—is a poetic device that most students, no matter how young, comprehend immediately and are able to use successfully. Anything nonhuman can be personified; often one of the simplest things for students to personify is the landscape around them. To illustrate this kind of personification, read the following poem and then have students point out the images that use personification.

Arkansas Night

In the Arkansas night
stars shimmer like cat's eyes.
Cows settle in the quiet fields
near silent sleeping tractors.
On porches, rocking chairs sigh
and swings sway a lullaby.
The house slumbers
as a clock pushes the dark away.
In the creek
a leaf tries to find the shore,
and a frog dances
from stone to slippery stone.

A barn owl winks as clouds
swallow the moon.

Sha'an Chilson
Arkansas Writers in the Schools

Almost every line in the above poem uses personification; by making the landscape and the things in it *come alive,* the descriptions become richer. This is concrete language taken a step further.

Now have the students write their own personification poems. Often, the name of the students' state or town, followed by a time of day, is the only prompt needed for the young writers to create lasting images of the places they live. Listed are some possible times of day to describe:

dawn	dusk
morning	evening
daybreak	nightfall
noon	midnight
afternoon	

The Door To . . .

Instruct the students to close their eyes. Tell them they are walking down a hallway. The hallway is full of doors, but all of the doors are closed. When they reach a door, tell them to stop. This is the door to winter. Tell them to slowly open the door and see what is inside. After instructing them to keep their eyes closed, call on a couple of the students and ask them to describe in detail what they see. After getting a few different descriptions, have the students keep their eyes closed while they close their doors and continue down the imagined hallway. At the end of the hallway is the door to summer. Now tell them to open the door, take a good look around, and then open their eyes and begin a poem titled "The Door to Summer," which describes what they experienced when they opened that door. As always, as many of the senses as possible should be used in this poem. Notice how the author of the following poem calls upon all the senses to describe the scene she is imagining.

The Door to Summer

As I open the door to summer,
I can see tiny mockingbirds flying about
the cool breeze, and I can smell little cherry blossoms
blooming, and I can hear the waterfall flowing
smoothly through the woods, and I can taste all the fruits
that are ripe, and as I walk I can feel the wind
blowing in my face.

Routh Standridge
Dover, Arkansas

The poem can be written as the door to any season. It is best, however, to pick a season other than the one that it actually is when the students do this exercise.

Synesthesia Poem

Synesthesia is a big word for a very simple idea. In a synesthesia poem, the students will use a certain sense to describe something that is usually described by using another sense. For instance, what sense do we usually use to describe thunder? Hearing, of course. But what would thunder *taste* like? Or *smell* like? A poem of this kind requires an immense amount of imagination and may stump students at first. It will probably be necessary to do a group poem. "Thunder" is a good word to start with. If students are having trouble, give them either/or choices. Would thunder be hot or cold? Probably hot. Now, hot like what? Like a baked potato, or like salsa? Would thunder be crunchy or chewy? Sweet or sour? After the group poem, list several possibilities on the board for students to choose from.

> What would snow sound like?
> What would laughter look like?
> What would thunder smell like?
> What would smoke feel like?
> What would a shadow taste like?

The students may use any sense that they wish, as long as it is not the sense with which they would usually experience that certain thing. In the following poem, synesthesia is used in a variety of ways. Ask the students if they can point out some examples.

Boy Observing Summer Storm

After sweet icicles melt in the sky,
vegetable greens taste like smeary tempera;
that hint of mist is meringue in his mouth.
Lost in a sticky scrap of naptime dream,
he hears the sour bang of the screen door,

> When the rain comes
> and washes away the green,
> redhead girls
> splash under their black umbrellas.

The moment aches like holding breath too long
while the clay sky molds to neighboring roofs.
The candy squeak of his new sneakers dissolves
in hot thunder. Noise darkens the room.
When thousands of sharp pins fall, he remembers,

The rain comes
and takes away the green.
Redhead girls
dance with their black umbrellas.

J'laine Robnolt
Arkansas Writers in the Schools

The author of this poem contends that vegetables can taste like paint, that the bang of a door can be "sour," that noise can "darken." Let your students make some contentions of their own; synesthesia is the perfect vehicle for a unique perspective on the world!

How to Know for Sure . . .

The "How to Know for Sure . . ." poem is an especially popular and successful exercise because it allows students to write about the things they are most familiar with in their lives. The best way to introduce this exercise is to write a group poem titled "How to Know for Sure You're in ——— (name of your town)." Give the students the following scenario: Some friends are driving cross country to visit you, but all the signs along the highways have mysteriously disappeared. How will your friends know for sure when they have reached your town? What are the sights, sounds, smells, et cetera that you can describe to the friends so they will know when to stop?

At first, students will give answers that are too general. They may say "there are lots of cows" or "you'll hear kids shouting on the playground." However, these things do not differentiate their town from thousands of others. Encourage them to be more specific.

How to Know for Sure
You're in Warren, Arkansas

The water tower, and the smell
from Bagit's pigpen. "Tomato town,"
pigeons and burned-out lights on the courthouse roof.
Teenagers drive like maniacs past the pine trees.
The wood mill smells like pine and smoke—
the whistle blows there every morning.

Ms. Johnson's class poem
Warren, Arkansas

Once the class poem has been written, and the students understand how important it is to be specific in this poem, they should write one of their own. Have index cards ready. On one side should be written "How to Know for Sure ———"; on the other side should be the topic of the poem. Here are some examples for topics:

How to know for sure
> you're at my school
> you're at my house
> you're in my grandmother's kitchen
> you're in my father's truck
> you're at the ballpark
> you're in my sister's room

Although places work well, the subjects of the poems should not necessarily be limited to identifying a location. The great thing about this poem is that possible topics are nearly limitless. Some successful ones are not about places:

How to know for sure
> the weather is going to turn bad
> it's time to go to bed

there are ghosts in your attic
you're dreaming
you watch too much television
you're about to get in trouble
you didn't do your homework
your dog is mad at you

The list could go on and on. As always, the more imaginative and specific the topics given, the better the poems will be.

How to Know for Sure
Your Retainer Is in the Trash

It's the cold chill of realization that washes over you
when your tongue hits the roof of your mouth
and nothing's there. It's the dread of your orthodontist's
probing look. It's knowing the napkin you so carefully
wrapped it in is at the bottom of the can,
buffeted by paper bags and milk cartons.
It's the cold scream of despair that runs through you
when your groping, frantic hand finds nothing.
It's the dragging of your feet back to class,
going over an array of stories to tell your mother
when you get off the bus.

Emmalee Carroll
El Dorado, Arkansas

Shape Poem

In this exercise, the students will attempt to write a poem that actually *looks like* what they are writing about. This can be done with line breaks, with white space between words, with creative punctuation, or (often) with all three. The following picture poem was originally done as a synesthesia exercise.

What Would a Tornado Taste Like?

A tornado may taste like bark or
wood from trees pulled from the ground,
or dingy from the dirt and mud. A tornado
may taste sweet from the corn picked
up, or like the meat of animals
caught up in it. A tornado
may taste like wool from sheep
or lambs, or wood, brick and
shingles from buildings
torn down. A tornado
may taste like plastic
metal from chairs
of a schoolhouse.
A tornado may
taste like
sorrow of
people
far &
near.

Karri Miller
Greenbriar, Arkansas

Obviously, the simpler the shape the easier the poem. A more difficult assignment would be to have the students write in the shape of a person, or an animal, as in this ambitious example:

```
                A
             horse.
          A horse
         is very
       beautiful as
     beautiful as
   a butterfly. It
  gallops and gallops
until it's done then
it look     s at everyone.
  Whe      n it's done, he'll give you a look that says hello
              everyone. Run, run, run until you're done. Gallop gal
           lop gallop gallop gallop gallop gallop gallop gallop gallo
          p drink drink drink drink drink drink drink drink drink dri
        nk drink eat eat eat eat eat eat eat eat eat eat eat eat eat eat eat
        look look look look look look look look look look look lo     ok look
         k ride ride ride ride ride ride ride ride ride ride ride ride      ride rid
         e ride hay hay hay hay hay hay hay hay hay hay hay hay h          ay hay h
        ay hay grass grass grass grass grass grass grass grass gras          s grass
        fence fence fence fence fence fence fence fence fence fe             nce fe
        nce fence fly fly fly fly fly fly fly fly fly fly fly fly fl            y fl
         y fly fly fl   y fly fly fly fly fly fly fly fly fly fly fly              fly
        white bl    ack yellow red maroon purple pink suns
        et white                        yellow red maro
        on purple                       pink sunset
        pony colt                       pony colt p
        ony co                          lt pony co
        lt fe                           nce gate h
        ay ea                           t grass f
        ly lo                           ok dr
        ink                             ride
        now                             now
        no                              w no
        w                               now
```

Bryce McWilliams
Hot Springs, Arkansas

Whatever shape they choose, remind students to keep in mind the rules of description and concrete imagery while working on this poem. It is easy for them to get carried away with their picture and forget to use the tools they have learned thus far. To make this poem truly successful, both the words and the picture must be able to capture the reader's attention.

Inside Poem

The inside poem calls for the students to make a shift in perspective. You will need index cards (one per student) for this exercise. On each card, write a noun. The catch is that the students must pretend they are small enough to be able to fit into such an object. Here are suggestions for specific objects:

watch	piano	cloud	shoe
soap bubble	ice cube	camera	candle
music box	popsicle	flashlight	star

Hand out one index card to each student, then ask the students, "What would it be like to be inside the object written on the card?" Go through the senses: What would they see, hear, touch, taste, smell?

Inside A Cactus

Inside, the moist pulp surrounds my body.
I can sense the presence of
tourists who have never seen me
and taste the blood on the fingers which have
     touched me.
The sunlight beats on my arms as
they bend towards the sky.
And the voice of the winds echo throughout
my stems and veins of life.

Larry McCain
West Memphis, Arkansas

Build-a-Title

Ask the students to name five adjectives (or you can say "describing words"). Encourage them to come up with interesting ones. "Pretty" or "good" or "dumb" are less interesting than, for instance, "sleepy" or "nervous" or "broken." Write the five adjectives in a column on the board. Now ask the students to come up with five nouns. Again, the more interesting the better. "Ape" is better than "book"; "flying saucer" is better than "hat." Write the nouns on the board in a second column beside the adjectives. You should now have two lists on the board. Perhaps they will be something like this:

sleepy	ape
nervous	flying saucer
blind	football
broken	reindeer
spotted	Trans Am

Now it's the students' turn. Tell them they must take one word from the first list, one word from the second list, and combine them. This will be the title of their poem, and the poem must be about the title they have created. For instance, this poem draws its title from the list above:

The Sleepy Reindeer

Christmas eve, sleigh packed tight
Santa walks quickly through the snow and the night.
He reaches the sleigh, where to his surprise
he's greeted by 14 reindeer eyes.
"Who's missing?" he shouts. His good cheer falls
as he marches to the reindeer stalls.
The baby reindeer dare not move;
they cover their eyes with their tiny hooves.

Then Santa finds what he's looking for:
in the last stall, Dasher's stretched out on the floor.
His tail is twitching, he's dreaming away;
his heavy snores gently scatter the hay.
"This is not the night for napping!"
Santa yells. "Now let's get cracking!"
So Dasher dashes to join the crew—
but he's still yawning over Katmandu.

This exercise gives the students a good deal of freedom; once they have chosen their title from the words on the board, the form and content of the poem are entirely up to them. The build-a-title exercise can also be a helpful start in generating short fiction.

Nursery Rhymes with a Twist

In this exercise, students will take common nursery rhymes and make them their own by changing either one or several elements of the original poems. Students almost always have something clever to add to the poems they choose to mimic. This exercise also offers students the chance to rhyme. Of course, their poems do not have to rhyme, but most students will stick to the original format of the nursery rhyme, changing just a few key words or ideas.

Little Miss Muffet

Little Miss Muffet sat on her tuffet
eating her chicken stew.
Along came a spider, he crawled up beside her,
and ended up squished on her shoe.

Mary Had a Little Lamb

Mary had a little lamb
whose fleece was white as snow.
Everywhere that Mary went
her lamb was sure to go.

She took the lamb to school one day.
The teacher screamed and yelled.
Mary and her little lamb
have now both been expelled.

Here are some other possible nursery rhymes to "twist":

    Humpty Dumpty
    Little Jack Horner
    Old Mother Hubbard
    Jack, Be Nimble
    Peter, Peter, Pumpkin Eater
    Little Bo-Peep
    Three Blind Mice
    Baa, Baa, Black Sheep
    Hey, Diddle, Diddle
    Hickory, Dickory, Dock
    Jack and Jill

4 ✏ Advanced

Dramatic Monologues

Dramatic monologues have the potential for being some of the most engaging and powerful poems students will write. They call for all the skills the students have learned up to this point. There are numerous variations involving the concept of the dramatic monologue. Following are four of the variations that will work best.

✏ Famous Person

In this exercise, you need to put the name of a famous person, animal, or character on each index card. Here are some suggestions:

Michael Jordan	Helen Keller
Amelia Earhart	George Washington
Cookie Monster	Pocahontas
Lassie	King Kong
Barney the Dinosaur	Superman
Paul Revere	Martin Luther King
Bugs Bunny	Tom Cruise
Frankenstein	

If you are working with younger students, you may have trouble coming up with enough "subjects" that will be recognizable to the students. If this is the case, you may have several students do the same subject. Obviously, the subjects you choose will depend on the ages of your students. Junior High students will probably not be interested in writing a "Barney" poem, but they may know more public figures than elementary students.

Instruct the students to imagine they are the subject on their card. They may write about anything, as long as the poem is in the voice of their subject. This may be a difficult concept for students, especially younger students, to grasp. Keep reminding them to think in terms of "I" rather than "he" or "she." It might be helpful to have them title their poems "I am ———(name of subject.)" If they have trouble finding a focus in the poem, suggest they write about what a typical day might be like for their subject.

✏ General Person

In this dramatic monologue, it is not necessary for the students to know any famous people, but imagination is vital. Think of different professions. Now, put an adjective in front of each profession, to give the students something to focus on in their poems.

> The Retiring Baseball Player
> The Surprised Race Car Driver
> The Sleepy Police Officer
> The Proud Doctor
> The Lazy Movie Star
> The Out-of-Tune Singer
> The Angry Math Teacher
> The Injured Dancer
> The Frightened Fire Fighter
> The Bored Mailman

Ask the students to imagine why these people are described by these adjectives and how this might affect their day. Again, make certain the students understand that the poem must be *from the subject's point of view.*

The Hobo Speaks

I watch the world pass me by.
No one watches me.
Beneath the piled up
stink and filth is a man.
Beneath all the dust and
worn out clothes is a heart.
Life seems to drag on,
dragging me behind it.
Searching in trash cans for food
becomes an adventure.
I notice everything,
but nobody notices me.

Samantha Hoover
Fort Smith, Arkansas

✏ Object

This poem is similar to the "inside poem," but this time the students get to *be* the object on the card. It should not be difficult to come up with topics for this poem; any noun will do. As always, though, the more interesting and specific the noun is the better the poem will be that comes from it.

In some aspects, this poem is more difficult than a dramatic monologue that is about a person or animal, because the students must be able to imagine that an object could have feelings. This technique, as stated earlier, is personification. Strangely, the older that students get, the less likely they are to easily accept the premise of this poem. Younger students, with more willing imaginations, should have no problem ascribing emotions to inanimate objects.

As before, if students are having trouble, suggest they imagine what a day in the life of this object might be like. Listed are some possible objects for this poem:

fire engine	saxophone
basketball	cookie jar
piano	textbook
gum	baseball bat
television	cotton candy
ferris wheel	pipe
bicycle	roller coaster

✏ Family Member or Friend

This dramatic monologue is much like the portrait poem but, again, calls for the students to write from a point of view other than their own. The dramatic monologue of a family member or friend can often be the most successful dramatic monologue that students write. The "day in the life" prompt will help this poem, as will encouraging the students to focus on senses, as they did in the portrait poems.

Headline Poem

The headline poem works especially well for older students, but can work with younger students as well if the headlines you choose are simple enough. The best place to find intriguing headlines is in supermarket tabloids. The ones which focus on celebrities are not as good; it is better to find ones that deal with extraordinary events in the lives of ordinary people.

> Woman Captured by UFO!
> Bigfoot Raids Grocery Store in Alaska!
> My Best Friend Is an Alien!
> Boy Born with Super Powers!
> Michael Jordan Was My Gym Teacher!

You can also use headlines from your local paper, although these probably will not be as interesting or appealing to students.

Cut out as many headlines as you need for all the students to have one. Hand out a headline to each student; the headline will be the title of the poem. The students can write the poems any way they wish, as long as the poems fit the titles. You may suggest ways to make an interesting poem. For instance, why not tell "Bigfoot Raids Grocery Store in Alaska!" from Bigfoot's point of view? How about writing "Boy Born with Super Powers!" from the point of view of the boy's mother? Often these poems will be silly, but they can be very effective, as in the following example.

Man Walks 100 Miles on His Hands

Legs straight, feet pointed
One step at a time.
Arms straining, sweat forming,
burning his eyes.
Looking ahead and down again.
Careful! Don't bend your waist!
Back straight, cramps forming,
pain spreading through every muscle.
Blisters rising, blisters popping,

blood showing through dirty brown bandage.
Slowly relax one muscle at a time.
Cramps and pain decreasing,
actually going to last.
Rome is ahead, the smell of
spring grass and sweet grapes
replacing the dust and mud
of the road.
Sore hands, painful arms,
pressure forming in his head.
Not now! he screams.
His mouth closed, no one hears.
The pain grows stronger,
copper taste in his mouth.
Something sticky, dripping from his ears.
Throbbing, pounding pain,
blood pooled and piled too long.
His nose now flows,
his heart is straining.
Collapsing, lying in the grass,
blood pooling around his head.
Just in time, bleeding slow.
He opens his eyes, smiling.
He survived 100 miles.

Laura S. Culp
Fort Smith, Arkansas

Litany

A **litany** is a poem that relies on the repetition of a
series of words for rhythm and emphasis. The concept of
the litany is simple, but it can produce some startling effects.

I Hear the Ocean

I hear the ocean that roars like a lion
I hear the ocean that moans at night
I hear the ocean that talks to me
I hear the ocean that is deeper than a pool
I hear the ocean that reads my mind
I hear the ocean that builds a wall
I hear the ocean
I hear the ocean that moves in motion
I hear the ocean that covers the world
I hear the ocean that knows the seashell
I hear the ocean that touches the sky
I hear the ocean that always waves
I hear the ocean that goes around and around

Phesonya Christian
Crawfordsville, Arkansas

The repetition, as well as the opportunity to look at a seemingly familiar object in a variety of different ways, makes this poem a favorite among students. It is especially effective with older students, although younger students may also create some memorable images in their descriptions. The litany can be about anything but should start with a personal pronoun followed by a verb. Often, as in the example, the senses work well. If a student is stuck on finding a topic, something in nature (plants, animals, etc.) often produces a successful litany.

Process Poem

The process poem is much like the recipe poem, but without the recipe format. You will need a set of index cards. On each card, write "How to," followed by an action of some kind. Tell the students to imagine they have to give a person who has never before done a simple practical procedure directions on exactly how to do it. Here are some possible titles:

> How to Dribble a Basketball
>
> How to Blow Out Candles on a Birthday Cake
>
> How to Make a Giant Sandwich
>
> How to Bathe the Dog

Writing about the above procedures or activities will help the students be specific and may produce some successful poems. However, the most successful process poems usually come from actions that are a little more sweeping (and a little more emotional) in nature.

> How to Fall in Love
>
> How to Annoy Your Brother or Sister
>
> How to Get in Trouble
>
> How to Win the Lottery
>
> How to Stay Up past Your Bedtime

You may make the process poems as strange and unlikely as you wish. You may be surprised how quickly the students begin writing after receiving index cards with more imaginative titles.

> How to Ride Your Bike on the Moon
>
> How to Eat Algebra
>
> How to Fly
>
> How to Walk on Hot Coals
>
> How to Keep a Shark in Your Bathtub

Here's a fine and funny example of an unlikely "how to":

How To Dig To China

You must pick your time carefully.
Wait until your mom frowns over the taxes
or your dog takes your dad for a walk.
Make three peanut butter and honey sandwiches.
Lick the knife: you can't get in trouble
in China. Then whistle your way outside.
Find the shadow of a hawk circling high up.
Mark it with an X. Lower your shovel
and start digging. Dig under the tulips
and the bones your dog buried.
Dig beneath the tunnels of gophers.
Crawl into your hole: now you should be
lower than the roots of the willow. Keep
Digging. Dig beneath the earthworm mud.
Dig through lava so hot the kernels
in your pockets burst into popcorn.
When you think you can't dig any longer,
You're almost there . . . See that faint
leak of light? It is the Chinese sun.
Far behind you is the moon. That echo?
It is your mother, calling you in for dinner.

Beth Ann Fennelly
Arkansas Writers in the Schools

Strange Best Friend Poem

What if your best friend were *algebra*? Or, what if your best friend were an orangutan? How about a planet? This is a fun poem that encourages students to use their imaginations and their skills in description. The exercise will require index cards; think of a strange best friend to write on each card. The friend doesn't have to be a living thing; some of the best, most imaginative poems will come from students who have the strangest best friends.

With older students, this poem can be modified to a "strange blind date" poem. Either way, the results are usually clever.

I Had a Date with Algebra II

I had a date with Algebra II. She gave
me directions to her house but I could
not understand them. I found the house
and went to the door. She had something
on that I had never seen before. We got in my
car and went to a movie she picked out.
I did not understand the plot and I felt
left out. We got in the car and she
started telling me about her life. That's
when I decided she should not be my wife.
I started to drive faster to get to her
house. She started to talk more. I
pushed the gas down to make the tires
squeal and just then I fell asleep at the wheel.

Jesse Morris
Prairie Grove, Arkansas

The "Crossing" Poem

This poem takes the personification poem a step further, by enlarging the landscape that the students must cover in their poems. The idea for the "crossing" poem comes from a work by Pulitzer Prize–winning poet Donald Justice:

Crossing Kansas by Train

The telephone poles
have been holding their
arms out
a long time now
to birds
that will not settle there
but pass with
strange cawings
westward to
where dark trees
gather about
a waterhole. This
is Kansas. The
mountains start here
just behind
the closed eyes
of a farmer's
sons asleep
in their workclothes.

Donald Justice

Like the personification poem, this poem offers students the opportunity to write about something they know well—their own homes. After reading the Justice poem to the students, tell them that they are going to write a poem about crossing their own state. It need not, however, be crossed by train. It could be crossed by foot, by bicycle, by car, or by airplane. Interestingly, some of the best crossing poems have come from the most unusual methods of crossing—by balloon, by shadow, by tractor, even by dream.

Crossing Arkansas by Dream

A car crawls
over the neverending
hills down to the valley
that has stretched
out for a nap,
the grass awaiting trees
that will not grow there,
and the sun sinks
sleepily beyond
the needlework
of the earth.

Kirsten Baldwin Metzger
Little Rock, Arkansas

What makes this poem and the Justice poem so successful is the way the inanimate worlds in each take on a
life of their own. The details used are specific and human.

Once your students have picked a method of crossing,
have them write the title of their poem: "Crossing ———
(their state) by ——— (their method)." Remind them to use
their senses as well as their tools of concrete and specific
language.

Crossing Arkansas on Horseback

The dust
from the roads
sticks to
the cars and the horses,
which are sweating
in the hot sun
as they trot down the road

towards new pastures
welcoming shade and rest
with the children and birds
under the apple trees.
They doze
in the midday heat
of an Arkansas summer.
But in the
evening
under the stars
the horses
come alive
and tear at the grass
with the moonlight
while the hushed chirping
of frogs echoes up
from the pond down the hill
and the children
sleep undisturbed.

Emilie Worthen
Little Rock, Arkansas

5 ✏ Fiction

Fiction in the Classroom

We are all storytellers by nature; every student who sits in your classroom knows what makes a good story and knows how to tell one. What is the first thing students do when they arrive at school each morning? They tell stories to their friends about what happened to them since they last saw each other. In order to keep their audience interested, they will focus on the most exciting parts of what transpired. They will avoid dull details and emphasize details that are funny, scary, or strange in some way. In keeping with the one-upmanship that is the rule in such situations, they might even exaggerate or embellish the truth. All these *skills* are the basis for writing fiction.

The teaching of fiction in the classroom poses a different challenge than the teaching of poetry. What makes fiction for students difficult is not the skill involved in creating it but simply the fact that writing a story usually takes more time than writing a poem. Any one of the poetry exercises in this book can be easily and successfully completed (and shared) within one class period. But usually the task of writing a complete short story will take more time. Younger students often have trouble with longer projects; their attention to a particular subject is likely to wane more quickly than older students' attention. What is offered here, then, is a brief overview of fiction techniques, followed by several exercises; these exercises will only occasionally produce complete stories, but they will consistently produce ground from which the students can build.

A question frequently asked by students is What makes fiction different than poetry? This is a complex question; many poems are in fact "stories" and could be written in prose. The most obvious difference between the two forms is that poems are told in lines and stanzas and stories are told in prose sentences and paragraphs. Another difference is that, because stories are usually longer than poems, there will be greater opportunity to develop a complex plot and well-rounded characters. Simply, the *scope* of a short story is often wider than that of a poem.

A story begins with two things: plot and character. Plot is what happens, and character is whom it happens to. These two elements must be woven together to form a story: plot cannot happen without character, and character cannot happen without plot. Two additional elements—dialogue and setting—enhance character and plot and should give the story a sense of immediacy and authenticity.

Plot

What is **plot**? Simply, plot is *what happens,* the sequence of events that makes up a story. Every plot contains some type of conflict that is illustrated to the reader through rising action and resolved (or, occasionally, not resolved) in a climax. Plot also includes motivation, which explains to the reader the *why* of the story in addition to the *what.*

A good way to introduce plot is to ask the students if they would like to see a motion picture in which two people sit on a park bench talking about themselves for two hours. Naturally, the students will say no. Why? Because it would be boring. Ask the students what they like best about their favorite movies. Most often the answer will be "action." This is the first lesson about plot: readers like action; they like to see things happen. It's important to point out to students that action does not necessarily mean what we think of when we hear the phrase "action movie." Action does not have to be car crashes, beatings, or explosions. Action does not have to be Arnold Schwarzenegger leaping out of a helicopter onto the roof of the Empire State Building. All those things are action, but action can also be someone running a race, someone moving out of a house, someone dancing in a restaurant, someone riding a horse. What action means, on its most basic level, is movement. If those people sitting on the park bench get up and walk around the park, the movie will be more interesting. If they ride the carousel while they're there, it will be more interesting still. And yet, none of these actions will be interesting if there is no conflict present. Perhaps the couple on the park bench is having an argument. Perhaps they are running from someone. Perhaps they are strangers dealing with a similar problem. Whatever the case, without conflict there can be no story.

Students, as a rule, have very little trouble with plot. Their classroom daydreams are so filled with exciting adventures that—given the opportunity—they will eagerly pour them out onto a page.

Character

Without strong **characters** in a story, the reader will have no one to identify with. People are what make plot happen, and creating original, fresh characters is essential to a story. A good way to get students to create interesting characters is to have them think about people in their own lives. Is everyone's father the same? Is everyone's grandmother the same? Of course not. No two people have *ever* been exactly the same, so no two characters should be either.

We all have attributes that make us unique; it is the writer's job to discover what it is that makes his characters unique. The most important thing to avoid when creating characters is clichés. If a student wants to write a story about a jet pilot, the student should strive to not make his character the clichéd jet pilot: a young, confident, brave, skillful, handsome man. A jet pilot could be a young woman. A jet pilot could be an on officer near retirement who fears he has lost his skills. A jet pilot could be an ordinary citizen with no experience who has been thrust into the role of defending his or her country.

A character, like a person, is made unique by tiny details. Even if the jet pilot is a confident young man, what if he has a pet mouse that he keeps in his breast pocket when he flies missions? What if his eyes are two different colors? What if he has a funny name? All these things will make this character come alive to a reader and, ultimately, will give the story life as well.

Dialogue

Dialogue is a direct quote of what a character says. Used properly, dialogue moves action forward while revealing character. Dialogue helps characters become real to readers. All people express ideas in different ways, and dialogue helps the reader to learn about the characters from the way they say something. Look at what we learn from these direct quotes:

> "I feel a bit under the weather."
> "I'm not feeling well."
> "I feel bad."
> "I don't feel so great."
> "I feel like garbage."

These quotes all convey the same information—the speaker doesn't feel well—but each one tells us something different about the speaker. We learn about people by listening to them talk; carefully chosen words in dialogue will bring the characters to life on the page.

Setting

Setting is important because it will help create an image (evoking *all* the senses) in the reader's mind of the places the characters inhabit. If students have worked with poetry, the element of setting will probably come easily to them, because it incorporates so many of the things used in poetry, mainly concrete language and sensory description. A reader wants to know what the world is like around the characters. It probably won't be necessary to describe each and every thing in a certain room, or to spend an entire paragraph talking about the appearance of the sky. But each time the setting changes in a story, the new setting should be established.

A writer should never screech the story to a halt in order to establish setting. This is avoided by establishing setting through action. It is dull to simply state, "In the room there was a brown chair, an old couch, and a rickety coffee table." Instead, the writer could say, "Matt plopped down in a brown chair. Bill sat down on an old couch and put his feet up on a rickety coffee table." By incorporating the setting into the action, the movement of the story does not stop.

The following is an example of a story, written by an eighth grader, that successfully uses plot, character, dialogue, and setting.

A Poor, Starry-Eyed Teenager

A poor, starry-eyed teenager worked in a run-down clam shack down by the pristine white sand on the beach of Florida. She was a relatively good waitress—always remembered to ask if they wanted dessert, always on time, never asked to switch shifts with other workers, kept her uniform nice and starched—but in her mind she was not a waitress. She was a dancer.

In her heart of hearts, she knew that to be ever truly happy she'd have to be living in the good ol' South doing what she wanted to do most in this world—square dancing.

One day she was flipping the TV from MTV to the football game the customers wanted to see when she saw—oh, she saw—a must-be message from God—on CMT (Country Music Television). Time was frozen, the music in the background faded, the cracking of clams couldn't be heard over her pounding heart, no one moved—shoot, no one breathed— while she gazed mesmerized by what she saw.

Beautiful, colorful, laughing ladies in huge, ruffled, checkerboard square skirts and tall, strong, slightly smiling men that spun them around the wooden floor with the greatest of pleasure and ease. Lights flickered and the melodic country twang surged in the background as a booming, hypnotizing voice called "CMT wants you, yes you to come to

Tennessee and try your fancy footwork at our big square dancing competition—cash prizes will be awarded to 1st, 2nd, 3rd places—call this number for more information."

Suddenly she was aware of the commotion around her—"Are you gonna change it to the game or what?" "We've already missed the kickoff, chick—hey, anybody home?" "Bring me a beer for the 50th time I say."

She was in a dream—her dream—she would be on CMT—she would square dance her secret country heart out. The ticket cost her over a month of her savings from working at the clam shack but she didn't care—she would live off the cash prizes she won from the contest—she would never come back to Florida.

She made a rural hoop skirt with some pieces of barbed-wire and covered it with beautiful red and white checked tablecloth. She brushed and curled her hair and applied her cosmetics in a way she thought most flattering to her delicate features and threw her scarcity of possessions in a paper grocery bag and walked briskly to the depot in her home-made square dancing skirt with visions of stardom filling her young head.

She handed the conductor her one-way ticket and asked him when she would need to change trains. She pressed the barbed-wire so close to her legs she felt blood and sweat trickle down her thighs as she made her way to the rear of the train. She sat back and closed her eyes, breathed deep her last smell of salt and mentally dosie-doed until she no longer heard the chugga-chug of the train.

Stacy Bennett
El Dorado, Arkansas

Notice how "A Poor, Starry-Eyed Teenager" begins with conflict (a waitress who does not like her job and dreams of being a dancer), then moves through rising action (seeing the announcement of the contest), to a climax (boarding the train to chase her dream). The author of this short piece also does a fine job of characterizing the young waitress, including telling details. Finally, dialogue and setting are also effectively used to move the story forward and give us a window into the character and her world.

It would be helpful to read this story aloud to students and then discuss how the author weaves all the elements of fiction together to make an entertaining, perhaps even moving, story.

Fiction Exercises

✏ Creating Inhabitants of Another Planet

This is a good exercise to introduce character and setting. Tell the students that a new planet has been found and that they are in charge of creating a new race of beings to live on this planet. Remind them to steer away from clichés—the inhabitants of their new race shouldn't be little green men with antennas on their heads. They can be anything—part animal, part human, part plant, part refrigerator—but they should be something original. Have the students write a paragraph describing the inhabitants. At first, they will want to focus mainly on physical description. That's a fine start, but encourage them to go beyond that. What are these beings like? What's the best job you can hold on this planet? What do these beings do in their spare time? What are families like? What is school like? With imagination, the possibilities are endless. In prose, as in poetry, the concrete details and specific descriptions the students choose to use will be the key in introducing their race of beings to the reader.

✏ Similar Elements Sketch

This is an effective exercise for showing students how everyone's imagination is different, even when certain elements of a story are the same. Tell the students they are going to write a scene about two people. Point to one student and ask, "Is the first character male or female?" Write this information on the board. Now ask another student, "How old is this person?" Again, write the information on the board. Go around the room asking other specific questions: What is the person's name? What does he or she do for a living? Now, move to character number two. Ask the same questions, again writing all the information on the board. When both characters are pinned down, pick someone to decide where the characters are. It doesn't matter at all: they can be in their backyard or on the moon. Finally, ask what they are discussing. Again, it can be anything, world peace or an infestation of ants. Now that all the information is on the board, instruct the students to write a scene with these two characters discussing whatever topic was decided upon. What will make these stories different? Two things: the details and the tone of the scene. Will the characters be angry or loving? Jealous or excited? These decisions are the ones left up to the students, and they will hopefully discover that these are the most important decisions of all. Even with these similar elements, all the students will come up with their own unique ideas of what transpires between the two characters.

✏ Luck of the Draw Story

This exercise will allow the students almost complete freedom in their writing. They may write a story about whatever they wish with, as usual, one catch. On index cards, (three per student) write nouns. Much like similar poetry exercises, the more interesting the nouns are, the better. After all the students have three cards, they may begin their stories. The only rule they have to follow is that they must fit the three nouns on their cards into their stories.

Just a few words can do wonders for getting students started on a story. This is made clear by the story that appears earlier in this section, "A Poor, Starry-Eyed Teenager," which grew from this exercise.

✎ Every Picture Tells a Story

There are two variations of this exercise. In the first variation, find a painting or photograph, in a magazine or book, that is big enough for all the students to see clearly if you walk around the room with it. It is best to find a picture that has only a few central people in it—even one person will do. The picture should involve some action, but it should not be anything overly dramatic (i.e., a plane crash). Instruct the students to tell the story behind the picture. Who are these people? How did they get where they are? What will happen next? Students may choose to focus on one aspect or several. Again, this exercise shows how we each interpret images and events differently. The elements may be the same, but the students' imaginations will create something that is uniquely theirs.

A variation on this exercise is to cut many pictures out of a magazine and have each student do a different picture. The students may paste or tape their pictures onto their paper and write their stories under them.

✎ Fairy Tales with a Twist

This exercise is much like the nursery rhyme with a twist, but it will take more than simply a clever rhyme or turn of phrase in order for it to be successful. The students should begin their stories as if they are simply recounting a common fairy tale. Before long, however, the tales should twist. Here are some examples:

> Cinderella gets lost on her way to the ball and ends up at a rock concert.
>
> The seven dwarves don't like Snow White.
>
> Little Red Riding Hood's grandmother is mean and the wolf has to save her.
>
> Goldilocks is an undercover agent; the three bears are suspected of bank robbery.
>
> The three little piggies are trying to eat the wolf. Will they snort and snort and blow the house down?

Like the nursery rhyme twists, this exercise is a favorite among students because it gives them a chance to add their voices to (and poke fun at) age-old stories. The results will usually be clever.

✏ Chain Story

This exercise will almost inevitably result in a nonsensical story, but students of all ages love it. The instructions for the chain story can be confusing and are most clear when defined step-by-step.

(1) Seat the students in a circle. Each student should have a sheet of paper.

(2) The teacher writes on the board one sentence that could begin a story. This sentence should be general and open-ended, for example, "I got lost while riding my bike on the outskirts of town" or "My friends and I took the bus to New York City."

(3) All students write this opening sentence on the top of their paper. Every student begins with this same sentence.

(4) After writing this opening sentence, all students pass their sheets to the right. At this point, students add a second sentence to the stories that are now in front of them. Students should then fold the top of the paper over everything that was written before their sentence. In other words, only the sentence just written should be visible.

(5) Then all the students pass their papers to the right again and each story continues. Each time students receive a new sheet of paper, they will add to that story and then fold down that sheet so that only their sentence is visible to the next writer.

(6) When the stories have completed the circle (or after a certain amount of time) have the students open up the sheets of paper and read the completed chain stories.

Usually, the stories will make no sense, but they will be funny. Occasionally, a coherent story finds its way through the chain.

Conclusion

The goal of teaching creative writing to students is not to produce professional poets and fiction writers. Instead, the goal is to help give students the skills and confidence necessary to express themselves through the written word. These skills in language will help students become better writers, better readers, and better thinkers.

In addition, creative writing can be an exciting process of self-discovery. In the classroom, this process can be heard clearly in the voices of children as they convey their unique perspectives of themselves, their families and friends, and the world around them. Being offered an outlet for this perspective may indeed be one of the greatest gifts a student ever receives.